Being:

Manifesting the Image of God

by

Garnet Nowell

Inspiration
Flows

Being:

Manifesting the Image of God

Garnet Nowell

Printed in the United States of America
First Printing: 2021

Published by Inspiration Flows
Broken Arrow, OK 74012
www.inspirationflows.com

Cover design: Copyright © 2021 CANVA

Introduction

Are you feeling down, doubtful, and afraid because you are not sure of who you are? Are you trying to 'find yourself'? Are you struggling to live up to someone's image of who you should be? It's time to realize that you are an image-bearer. You were made in His image and likeness. God created you to BE! Being is about coming to terms with your Godly image. God sees you; be true to what God has called you to do and to be and know that He is always on your side as you continue to grow into perfection.

We are *progressively* being transformed into His image from [one degree of] glory to [even more] glory, which comes from the Lord, [who is] the Spirit (2 Corinthians 3:8)

Enjoy the journey.

Be Enough:
Wonderfully Made

God made you a unique being.
You are and always will be enough.
Never let anyone tell you that you are not
ENOUGH.

"I will give thanks and praise to You,
for I am fearfully and wonderfully made;
Wonderful are Your works,
And my soul knows it very well."

Psalm 139:14

Be Adventurous:
Purpose Driven

You were created for a purpose.
Ask God to show you, and He will. You
were not created to walk through
your life without a clue; God has plans
for you.

"For I know the plans *and* thoughts that
I have for you,' says the Lord, 'plans for
peace *and* well-being and not for disaster,
to give you a future and a hope."

Jeremiah 29:11

Be Beautiful:
God Made You
Beautiful in His Time

There is nothing more beautiful
than a woman who chooses to obey God.
Trust Him to bring beauty into your life
even when things appear at their darkest.

"He has also planted eternity [a sense of
divine purpose] in the human heart [a
mysterious longing which nothing
under the sun
can satisfy, except God]"

Ecclesiastes 3:11

Be Content:
Lacking Nothing

You are important to God.
He will supply your every need.
Trust Him.

He said, "I will never [under any
circumstances] desert you [nor give
you up nor leave you without support,
nor will I in any degree leave you
helpless], nor will I forsake or
let you down or relax
My hold on you [assuredly not]!"

Hebrews 13:5

Be Courageous:
Run to the Battle

War will come,
you must learn to fight.
Fear not; let Faith guide you.
Use your spiritual weapons. Remember,
your weapons are much greater and
stronger than those of the enemy.

The weapons of our warfare
are not of flesh but have
divine power to destroy strongholds.

2 Corinthians 10:4 (ESV)

Be Teachable:
Learning is Loving

Be mindful that you do not know
everything. You only have a small part
to play in this earthy drama.
Remain teachable.

Whoever loves instruction and
discipline loves knowledge,
But he who hates reproof and
correction is stupid.
Do not be stupid.

Proverbs 12:1

Be Humble:
It's Not About You

Do not *merely* look out for your own
personal interests, but also for
the interests of others. Remember, Love
God, Love Neighbors, Love Yourself.

Each of us leads busy lives.
In our daily walk, pursue God's
agenda and search for
someone who needs your help. There is
someone out there waiting for you to obey
and offer to help. Live and love
sacrificially.

Philippians 2:4

Be Present:
Guard Your Moments

In His presence there is fullness of joy.
Be ever-present in the time
you have been given each day. You
have 24 hours, 1,440 minutes each day
to utilize. Don't waste it.

Do not hide from the fiery arrows of
the enemy; be on guard. God is with you,
and the enemy is a defeated foe.

1 Corinthians 16:13

Be Sober:
Leading Change

We are filled with purpose. We are strong
and courageous, and we run toward our
battles. Yet, on the inside we are self-
controlled, calm, and wise.

We are clothed with the breastplate
of faith and love, and as a helmet, we are
covered with the hope *and* confident
assurance of salvation.
We will not back
down, nor will we quit.

1 Thessalonians 5:6-8

Be Vigilant:

Preparation is Never Lost Time

We must be alert and cautious at all times. The enemy is prowling, looking, and checking every corner of your life looking for ways to attack and devour you.

Do not let your guard down. Always be ready to counter his attacks with spiritual weapons.

Prepare, prepare, prepare!

1 Peter 5:8

Be Free:
Looking Toward Eternality

*Rejoice in the Lord. Christ set us free
[completely liberating us], no more
bondage, no more fear, no more chains,
and no more shame. This is a truth we
must know if we are to
remain free.*

*God has called you to a free life. Just make
sure that you don't use this freedom as an
excuse to do whatever you want to do and
destroy your freedom.
Rather, use your freedom to serve
one another in love.*

Galatians 5:1 (MSG)

Be Confident:
Finish Strong

Our confidence is in Jesus. Confidence
should ooze out of every pore in
your body.
The enemy should smell that confidence
before he gets within stalking
distance of you.
We are sure of this, and we are also
confident that Jesus will (by His power)
finish the good work He started in us. He
will keep
working on perfecting us until the
time of His return.
Count on it.

Philippians 1:6

Be Ready:
Entering into His Presence

*Take care. Jesus is coming back, and you
need to be ready. He will come as
a thief in the night so therefore keep the
faith, do not stray from His care.*

*Only those who have called
on Him will be saved.
The bridegroom awaits His bride.
Are you ready to enter into
His presence?*

Matthew 25:10-13

Be Equipped:
Unity in the Faith

We are fully equipped *and perfected for* works of service. We know Him and are becoming more thoroughly acquainted with Him, by being *continually* conformed inwardly into His likeness.

We are manifesting His image in spiritual completeness as we grow in the unity of faith.

Ephesians 4:12-13

Be Thankful:
Forever Grateful

Always give thanks to God the Father
for all things, in the name of our Lord
Jesus Christ.
We must be forever grateful
for all He has and will do for us.

Praying continually without anxiety or
worry about every situation knowing
when we make our petitions known
He hears us.

Philippians 4:6

Be Encouraged: Leaving the 99

We can have perfect peace knowing that Jesus would leave the 99 and come in search of us. Be of good courage; God loved us so much that He gave His greatest gift (Jesus) so that we might have life and life more abundantly.
Jesus has overcome the world.
In Me you may have [perfect] peace.
In the world you have tribulation and distress and suffering, but be courageous [be confident, be undaunted, be filled with joy]; I have overcome the world."

John 16:33

Be Healed:
Breaking Free

*We have been wounded, beaten down,
broken, and thrown away. But Jesus!
He willingly took all our pain
and sorrow so that we may be totally
healed.*

*He willingly offered Himself on an altar
of sacrifice. It was for freedom that
Christ set us free.
Hold on to your healing,
no matter the struggle.*

1 Peter 2:24

Be Faithful:
Drawing Near

*Have a constant faith in God because
without faith it is impossible to
[walk with God and] please Him.*

*He rewards those who [earnestly
and diligently] seek Him. Keep seeking
Him, keep asking Him, continually draw
nearer to Him. Abide in Him. He sees you
and knows everything about the road
you had to travel to reach Him.*

Hebrews 11:6

Be Wise:
Get Understanding

Do you want to know how to succeed?
It's no secret.
Ask God and get skillful and godly wisdom.
Acquire understanding by actively
seeking spiritual discernment, mature
comprehension, and logical interpretation.

Pay attention [and be willing to learn] so
that you may gain
understanding *and* intelligent
discernment.
God will give it to you generously.
I promise.

Proverbs 4:5

Be Spirit-filled: Overflowing

Drinking wine and getting drunk is corruption and stupidity. Instead, be forever filled and overflowing with the Spirit of God.

Allow the Holy Spirit to give you the ability to communicate with a spiritual language.

Do not hold back, let your new language flow out of you like rivers of living water.

That beautiful language is your gateway to the Supernatural!

Ephesians 5:18

Be Prosperous:
Encompassing Wholeness

God's promise. You who fear and trust in the Lord. He is your help and your shield. The Lord is thinking of you constantly, and He will bless you. The Lord will give you increase more and more.

Prosperity is a wholeness word. It encompasses wealth, health, and freedom from sin. Learn to love it and to embrace it.

Psalm 115:11-16

Be Steadfast:
Abounding in All Things

Be steadfast, immovable, always excelling in the work of the Lord [always doing your best and doing more than is needed], being continually aware that your labor [even to the point of exhaustion] in the Lord is not futile nor wasted [it is never without purpose].

You will be blessed if you wait patiently and stand up under temptation. God has promised the victor's crown to those who love Him.

1 Corinthians 15:58
James 1:12

Be Prudent:
Silence Cannot Be Misquoted

Be prudent and discreet and not naïve.
Do not be easily misled by believing
everything you hear. Consider the source.

Look ahead and be prepared for what's
coming. God will hide and protect
you in the shadow of His wings if
you are prudent. Don't suffer the
consequences of being naïve and
fall into sin.

Proverbs 14:15
Proverbs 22:3

Be Forgiving:
Reciprocal Agreements

Jesus said to forgive 'seventy by seven'. He meant, always forgive. It's not for the other person, it's for YOU.

Get out there and walk—better yet, run!—on the road God called you to travel. Don't sit around on your hands or stroll off down some path that goes nowhere. Instead, do this with humility and discipline. Pour yourselves out for each other in acts of love, alert at noticing differences, and quick at mending fences.

Ephesians 4:3

Be Generous:
Sowing Your Future Harvest

Give [thoughtfully and with purpose] as you have decided in your heart, not grudgingly or under compulsion, for God loves a cheerful giver [and delights in the one whose heart is in his gift].

It is more blessed [and brings greater joy] to give than to receive. So, give away your life; you'll find life given back, but not merely given back—given back with bonus and blessing.

Generosity manifests generosity.

2 Corinthians 9:7

Luke 6:38

Be Sanctified:
Purposeful Living

You were created by God for a
specific purpose. Live it out.
Take your everyday, ordinary life—your
sleeping, eating, going-to-work, and
walking-around life—and place it before
God as an offering.
Don't become so well-adjusted to your
culture that you fit into it without even
thinking. Instead, fix your attention on
God. You'll be changed from the inside out.
God brings the best out of you and
develops well-formed maturity in you.

Romans 12:1

Be Kind:
Sweetness Prevails

Put on a heart of compassion, kindness, humility, gentleness, and patience [which has the power to endure whatever injustice or unpleasantness comes your way.

Let the peace of Christ be the controlling factor in your hearts [deciding and settling all questions that arise].

Instruct and direct one another using good common sense. And sing, sing your hearts out to God! Let every detail in your lives—words, actions, whatever—be done in the name of the Master, Jesus, thanking God the Father every step of the way.

Colossians 3:12

Be Patient:
Looking Toward the Promise

Let the Holy Spirit produce this kind of fruit in your lives: love, joy, peace, patience, kindness, goodness, faithfulness, gentleness, and self-control. There is no law against these things!

Do not allow yourselves to get fatigued doing good. At the right time, you will harvest a good crop if you do not quit. Instead, with all humility [forsaking self-righteousness], and gentleness [maintaining self-control], and with patience, bear with one another in unselfish] love.

Galatians 5:22-23; 6:9

Be Inspired:
Every Breath

All Scripture is God-breathed [given by divine inspiration] and is profitable for instruction, for conviction [of sin], for correction [of error and restoration to obedience], for training in righteousness [learning to live in conformity to God's will, both publicly and privately— behaving honorably with personal integrity and moral courage].

God planted a seed within us. When we water that seed with the living waters of the Word and prayer, it grows. Be inspired by that growth.

2 Timothy 3:16

Be Transformed: Embracing Change

Do not be conformed to this world [any longer with its superficial values and customs] but be transformed and progressively changed [as you mature spiritually] by the renewing of your mind [focusing on Godly values and ethical attitudes], so that you may prove [for yourselves] what the will of God is, in His plan and purpose for you.

He knows the plans He has for you. Embrace all that He has, and you will find good success.

Romans 12:2

Be Tenacious:
Holding on to the Promise

So let us seize *and* hold fast *and* retain
without wavering the hope we
cherish *and* confess *and* our
acknowledgment
of it, for He Who promised is reliable
(sure) *and* faithful to His Word.

We cannot lose faith. We must be like a
starving dog, which holds onto the bone he
found. The same tenacity, holding on to
your faith, will keep you strong in the
midst of any and every circumstance.

BE TENACIOUS!

Hebrews 13:23

Be Prayerful:
Always Thankful

Do not fret or have any anxiety about anything, but in every circumstance and in everything, by prayer and petition (definite requests), with thanksgiving, continue to make your wants and needs known to God.

He bends down to listen, therefore pray as long as you have breath. If you see trouble and sorrow, Call on the name of the LORD.

Philippians 4:6
Psalm 116:2-4

Be Content:
Expect Great Rewards

Be content in all things, contentment has great rewards. Do not covet what you see others have obtained. Walk in obedience and watch God bless you beyond measure.

God is faithful because He has promised us in His Word. Remember, He is not a man therefore He cannot lie. If He said it, EXPECT IT to come to pass.

Faith begins where the will of God is known, so become familiar with His Word, His will.

1 Timothy 6:6-11

Be Joyful:
An Offering of Praise

In His presence is fullness of joy and pleasures forevermore.

When you enter His courts with an offering of praise, all your worries are carried away.

Weeping may endure for just a little while, but joy will come flowing back to you.

Make a joyful noise, sing a song unto the Lord. For the Lord is GOOD, and His mercy is everlasting!

Psalm 16:11

Psalm 100

Be Ready:
Lift Up Your Eyes

Wait patiently for His return.
Continue to walk worthy of
the sacrifice which was made for you.

Follow the greatest of all
commandments:

Walk in Love.
Love God with all you have;
love your neighbor as yourself;
and love your enemies.

Love covers a multitude of sins.
Practice Kingdom Living.

1 Peter 4:8

Books by Garnet Nowell

Hey, Don't Be That Girl
21-Day Devotional

Hey, Don't Be That Girl
Devotional Journal

Praying Through the Pandemic: Ignite
Your Faith, Conquer Your Fear

Want more inspiration? Visit my blog:
Inspiration Flows

@ www.inspirationflows.com

Follow me on Facebook, LinkedIn

Meet the Author!

Garnet Nowell is an author, Christian blogger, mom, and educator. Her brand is Inspiration Flows, and she inspires others to pursue their purpose with passion. Garnet grew up in Edenton, North Carolina. She attended college at North Carolina Central University earning a bachelor's in business education. She also earned a master's in theology from Oral Roberts University and a master's in Library and Information Studies from the University of Oklahoma. She is currently working on her Doctorate in Educational Leadership at Oral Roberts University.

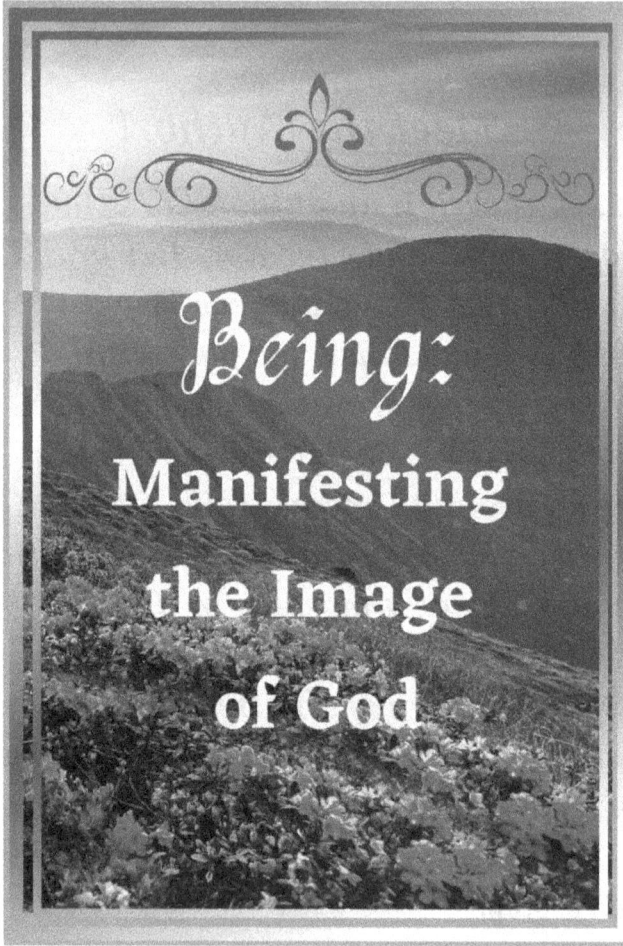

Being:
Manifesting
the Image
of God

www.ingramcontent.com/pod-product-compliance
Lightning Source LLC
Chambersburg PA
CBHW060100050426
42448CB00011B/2561